Delaware Water Gap National Recreation Area and Upper Delaware Scenic and Recreational River

Weather of 2009

Natural Resource Data Series NPS/ERMN/NRDS—2010/083

Paul Knight, Tiffany Wisniewski, Chad Bahrmann, and Sonya Miller

Pennsylvania State Climate Office
503 Walker Building
Pennsylvania State University
University Park, Pennsylvania

September 2010

U.S. Department of the Interior
National Park Service
Natural Resource Program Center
Fort Collins, Colorado

The National Park Service, Natural Resource Program Center publishes a range of reports that address natural resource topics of interest and applicability to a broad audience in the National Park Service and others in natural resource management, including scientists, conservation and environmental constituencies, and the public.

The Natural Resource Data Series is intended for timely release of basic data sets and data summaries. Care has been taken to assure accuracy of raw data values, but a thorough analysis and interpretation of the data has not been completed. Consequently, the initial analyses of data in this report are provisional and subject to change.

All manuscripts in the series receive the appropriate level of peer review to ensure that the information is scientifically credible, technically accurate, appropriately written for the intended audience, and designed and published in a professional manner. This report received informal peer review by subject-matter experts who were not directly involved in the collection, analysis, or reporting of the data. Data in this report were collected and analyzed using methods based on established, peer-reviewed protocols and were analyzed and interpreted within the guidelines of the protocols.

Views, statements, findings, conclusions, recommendations, and data in this report do not necessarily reflect views and policies of the National Park Service, U.S. Department of the Interior. Mention of trade names or commercial products does not constitute endorsement or recommendation for use by the U.S. Government.

This report is available from Eastern Rivers and Mountains Network (http://science.nature.nps.gov/im/units/ERMN) and the Natural Resource Publications Management website (http://www.nature.nps.gov/publications/NRPM).

Please cite this publication as:

Knight, P., T. Wisniewski, C. Bahrmann, and S. Miller. 2010. Delaware Water Gap National Recreation Area and Upper Delaware Scenic and Recreational River: Weather of 2009. Natural Resource Data Series NPS/ERMN/NRDS—2010/083. National Park Service, Fort Collins, Colorado.

NPS 620/105524, 647/105524, September 2010

Table of Contents

Figures

Tables

List of Key Acronyms

COOP   National Weather Service Cooperative Observer Program

CWOP   Citizen Weather Observer Program

DEWA   Delaware Water Gap National Recreational Area

ERMN   Eastern Rivers and Mountains Network

FAA   Federal Aviation Administration

GOES   Geostationary Operational Environmental Satellite

IFLOWS   Integrated Flood Observing and Warning System

NADP   National Atmospheric Deposition Program

NARR   North American Regional Reanalysis

NCDC   National Climatic Data Center

NOAA   National Oceanic and Atmospheric Administration

NWS   National Weather Service

NRA   National Recreation Area

PDSI   Palmer Drought Severity Index

POR   Period of Record

PRISM   Parameter-elevation Regressions on Independent Slopes Model

RAWS   Remote Automated Weather Stations

SRR   Scenic and Recreational River

UPDE   Upper Delaware Scenic and Recreational River

USDM   United States Drought Monitor

USGS   United States Geological Survey

Introduction

Weather and climate are widely recognized as key drivers of terrestrial and aquatic ecosystems, affecting biotic as well as abiotic ecosystem characteristics and processes. Global and regional scale climatic patterns, trends, and variations are critical to the cycling of elements, nutrients, and minerals through the ecosystems and can deliver pollutants from regional and even global sources (National Assessment Synthesis Team 2001). These variations and trends influence the fundamental properties of ecologic systems such as soil-water relationships and plant-soil processes and their disturbance rates and intensity. Information obtained from meteorological monitoring will be useful to interpreting and understanding changes in species composition, community structure, water and soil chemistry, and related landscape processes (Marshall and Piekielek 2007).

The purpose of this report is to provide a concise weather and climate summary for the period from January 1 through December 31, 2009 and to place current patterns and trends in an appropriate historical and regional context (Knight et al., in preparation). It is our intention that this report will satisfy an inherent interest in meteorological phenomena and meets a portion of the Eastern Rivers and Mountains Network (ERMN) Weather and Climate Monitoring objectives:

- Document long-term trends in weather and climate through seasonal and annual summaries of selected parameters (e.g., multiple forms of precipitation, temperature).
- Identify and document extremes and averages of climatic conditions for common parameters (e.g., precipitation, air temperature) and other parameters where sufficient data are available (e.g., wind speed and direction, solar radiation).
- Provide information on near real-time weather parameters, historical climate patterns, and climate station metadata from a single, easy-to-use Internet portal.

To accomplish these objectives, a variety of atmospheric data streams were evaluated for their quality, longevity, and applicability to the ERMN parks. Since no single weather observing network contains all the pertinent measures of atmospheric phenomena to assess ecosystem health, an objective analysis of the data networks was developed and outlined in the Weather and Climate Monitoring Protocol for the Eastern Rivers and Mountains Network and the Mid-Atlantic Network of the National Park Service (Knight et al., in preparation). Through this analysis, a select number of weather/climate observing stations were chosen as representative of each park; these are the primary data sources used to profile climate summary and trends.

In addition to a suite of summary tables, graphs, and narratives, we specifically identify a series of key climatological indicators to report status and trends on an annual basis and periodically in separate and more thorough reports. These key indicators are further described in the protocol (Knight et al., in preparation) and summarized in this report.

Climate of the Pocono Mountains and Eastern Plateau

Delaware Water Gap National Recreation Area (NRA) lies in Pennsylvania Climate Division 1 "Pocono Mountains" and New Jersey Climate Division 1 "Northern NJ," while Upper Delaware Scenic and Recreational River (SRR) lies within Pennsylvania Climate Division 1 and New York Climate Division 2 "Eastern Plateau." A climate division is a region that is reasonably homogenous with respect to climatic and hydrologic characteristics and is frequently used for compiling climate statistics http://www.esrl.noaa.gov/psd/data/usclimate/map.html). Pennsylvania and New York are each divided into 10 climate divisions; New Jersey has three divisions.

The three climate divisions encompassing Delaware Water Gap NRA and Upper Delaware SRR are generally considered to have a humid, continental type of climate, but the varied physiographic features have a marked effect on the weather and climate of the various parts of the Delaware River valley. The prevailing westerly winds carry most of the weather disturbances that affect the region from the interior of the continent, so that the Atlantic Ocean has limited influence on the climate of the area (Davey et al. 2006). Coastal storms do, at times, affect the day-to-day weather, especially in the winter. Also, storms of tropical origin can have the greatest effect within this portion of the Pennsylvania–New Jersey–New York region, causing severe floods in some instances (Gelber 2002).

Temperatures are moderately continental, with the tempering effects of the Great Lakes contributing to cloud production in the winter and onshore winds reducing the heat at times during the summer. The lowest readings in the winter occur with polar air masses of Canadian origin settling over the Northeast after a fresh snowfall. The highest readings of the summer happen when the sub-tropical fair weather system, the Bermuda high, pushes westward into the Carolinas. Its clockwise circulation will direct hot, humid air from the Gulf region into the Delaware River valley. The southwest winds gain additional warmth when descending the crest of the Appalachians.

Precipitation is fairly evenly distributed throughout the year. Annual amounts generally range between 34–52 in (864–1,320 mm), while the majority of places receive 38–46 in (965–1,168 mm). Greatest amounts usually occur in the late-spring and summer months; while February is the driest month, having about 2.0 in (51 mm) less than the wettest months. Precipitation tends to be somewhat greater in the mountains, due primarily to coastal storms which occasionally frequent the area. During the warm season these storms can bring heavy rain, while in winter, heavy snow or a mixture of rain, ice, and snow may be produced.

Surface winds blow from the west and northwest in the cold season and from the southwest during the warm half of the year. Thunderstorms follow a frequency that matches the solar cycle, occurring between the equinoxes and reaches a peak near the summer solstice. Hail is relatively infrequent, but flash floods and damaging thunderstorm winds affect parts of the river valley each summer. On average, tornadoes pass through the area about once every three years. The direct effects of an Atlantic hurricane are uncommon, though remnant rains from hurricanes and tropical storms have contributed to the region's worst floods. Ice storms, which can cause significant disruption, occur at irregular intervals and are primarily confined to the months between December and March (Kocin and Uccellini 2004).

Observing Stations

A total of 25 weather observing stations comprised of six observing networks were selected around Delaware Water Gap NRA and Upper Delaware SRR. Representative stations within a 100-km range of each park were chosen based on several criteria, which include proximity to the park, the representativeness of the station to the park elevation profile, the type and frequency of observations, the period of record of the data, and data availability (Knight et al., in preparation). A subset of these observing networks (IFLOWS, GOES, NADP, and CWOP; 10 total stations) are not yet utilized for these reports due to limited data availability and/or lack of data quality assurance (Bureau of Land Management 1997). Moreover, the percentage of time a station reports particular parameters (e.g., temperature) can influence its data inclusion. Three stations were excluded in 2009 based upon this criterion. Therefore, a total of 12 stations were used for this report (Figure 1, Table 1).

In addition to the summary information available in this report, a near real-time data stream has been made available to the ERMN through a Web interface for the selected stations along with monthly, seasonal, and annual summaries. The Web interface is accessible through the following link: http://climate.met.psu.edu/gmaps/NPS_DEVELOPMENT/interface.php.

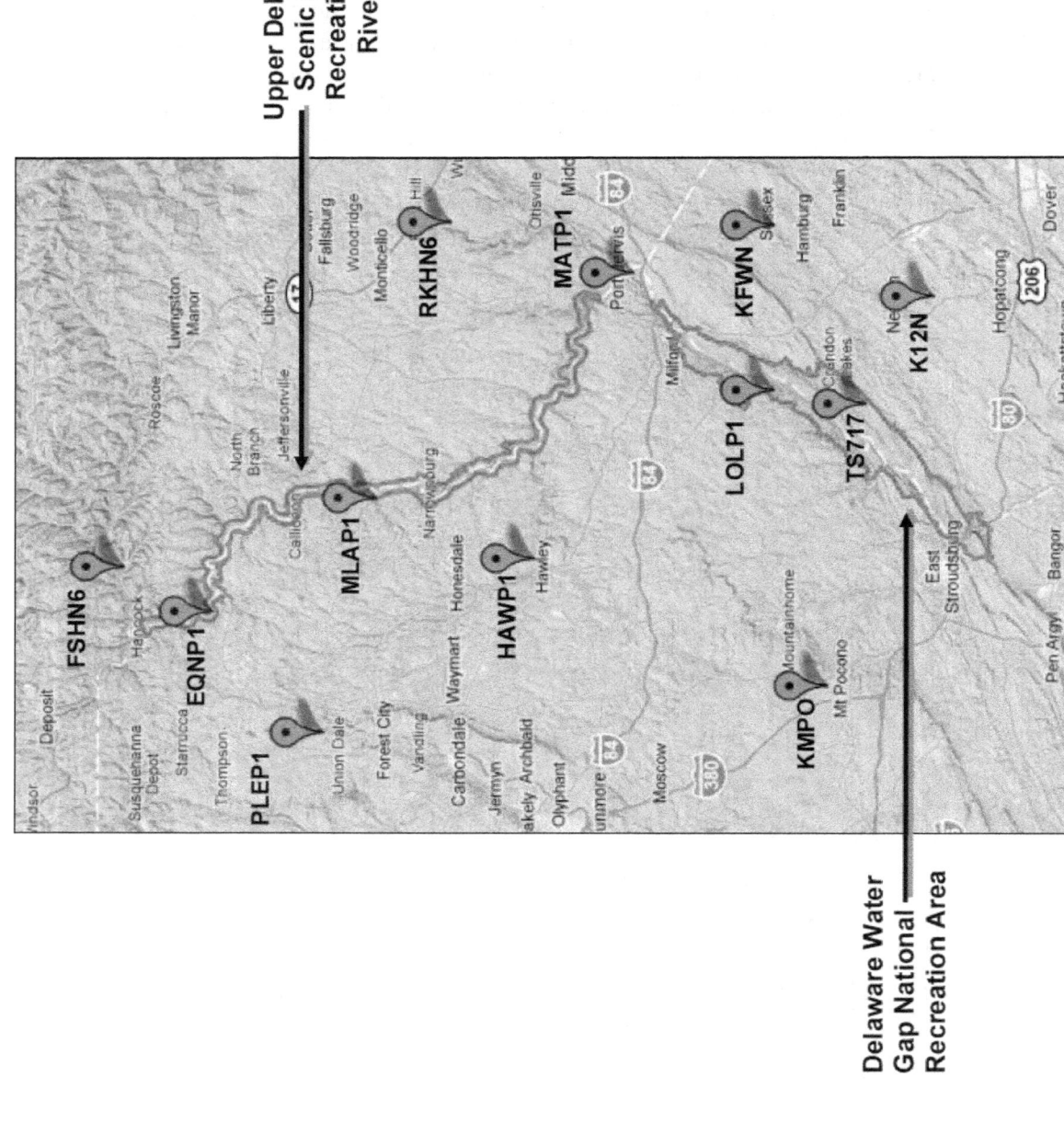

Figure 1. Location of weather observing stations around Upper Delaware SRR and the Delaware Water Gap NRA.

4

Table 1. List of weather observing stations around the Upper Delaware SRR and the Delaware Water Gap NRA selected as most representative of the parks in 2009.

Station	Observing Network	Station Name	Period of Record (POR)		Percentage of Time Reporting Temperature for 2009	Percentage of Time Reporting Precipitation for 2009	Percentage of Time Reporting Temperature for entire POR	Percentage of Time Reporting Precipitation for entire POR
MATP1	COOP	Matamoras	10/01/1904	Present	100.0	100.0	90.7*	94.4
EQNP1	COOP	Equinunk 2 NW	03/01/1957	Present	-	100.0	-	99.2
HAWP1	COOP	Hawley 1 E	11/01/1897	Present	99.7	100.0	74.1	80.0
RKHN6	COOP	Rock Hill 3 SW	06/01/1963	Present	99.5	96.4	99.7*	98.4
FSHN6	COOP	Fishs Eddy	11/13/2006	Present	-	77.5	-	47.6
KMPO	FAA	Mount Pocono	09/29/1999	Present	99.4	99.4	98.5	98.7
KFWN	FAA	Sussex	12/27/2000	Present	97.0	97.0	99.3	99.3
K12N	FAA	Andover	10/25/2000	Present	97.0	97.0	80.0	80.0
PLEP1	COOP	Pleasant Mount 1W	10/01/1924	Present	100.0	99.7	98.3*	97.9
MLAP1	COOP	Milanville	08/01/1945	Present	83.3	83.3	51.7*	42.5
TS717	RAWS	Blue Mountain Lakes	12/11/2007	Present	98.1	98.1	94.7	94.7
LOLP1	RAWS	Loch Lomond	01/01/2005	Present	99.5	99.5	94.7	94.7

* Matamoras did not start reporting temperature until 07/01/1963. The percentage time of reporting temperature is based upon this por.
* Rock Hill 3 SW did not start reporting temperature until 12/01/2008. The percentage time of reporting temperature is based upon this por.
* Pleasant Mount 1 W did not start reporting temperature until 12/01/1951. The percentage of time reporting temperature is based upon this por.
* Milanville did not start reporting temperature until 06/20/1963. The percentage of time reporting temperature is based upon this por.

5

Temperature Summary

Calendar year 2009 averaged below the long-term mean temperature (Table 2), with maximum temperatures departing between -0.5 and -2.3 degrees Fahrenheit (°F) (-0.2 and -1.2 degrees Celsius [°C]) for the year. Minimum temperature readings averaged closer to the 30-year mean (Table2). January 2009 was colder than normal, but February, March, and April had above-average temperatures (Figures 2 and 3). The maps in Figures 2 and 3 were created using estimates from the Parameter-elevation Regressions on Independent Slopes Model (PRISM). PRISM uses an interpolation scheme for temperature between actual observations and corrects these estimates for changes in topography across the region (Daly et al. 2002). More information can be found at http://www.prism.oregonstate.edu/.

Pleasant Mount, PA, which is near Upper Delaware SRR, had an average monthly temperature of 14.0°F (-10.0°C) for January, 2009 (Table 3). This was 4.9°F (2.7°C) below the average (Table 4). Several cold episodes brought morning readings well below 0°F (-17.8°C) during January, with the lowest values in many sections occurring at mid-month with minima between -12 and -15°F (-23.5 to -25.5 (°C)). The number of sub freezing nights varied, with Matamoras accruing more than average, but Pleasant Mount tallying fewer than normal (Table 2).

The spring began milder than normal and concluded cooler than average, with the period April–May–June averaging above the long-term mean (Figures 2 and 3; Tables 3 and 4). For example, Pennsylvania Climate Division 1 "Pocono Mountains," which encompasses most of Upper Delaware SRR and Delaware Water Gap NRA, ranked as the 27th warmest spring in the past 115 years (57 is the mid-point; Table 5). At the same time, Delaware Water Gap NRA, which also resides in the New Jersey Climate Division 1 "Northern NJ," ranked as the 30th warmest spring since 1895 (Table 5). Cloud cover contributed to bouts of unseasonably cool weather during June. Some sections had a late freeze and frost (between May 19–20), though most areas marked their last hard freeze on April 25. Temperatures during June had large negative daytime departures, with readings between 0.6 and 3.0°F (0.3 and 2.3°C) below normal (Figure 2; Table 4). A warm spell came early when temperatures rose to 86°F (30°C) between May 21–23.

The summer period was cooler than average due to persistent cool weather during July (Figure 2; Tables 3 and 4). No record maximums were recorded during July, August, and September. The longest warm spell occurred from August 15–27 when readings regularly rose into the 80s°F (28–32°C).

Autumn temperatures were well above average (Tables 3 and 4; Figures 2 and 3). Frosts and freezes occurred near the long-term average, with most sections noticing sub-freezing readings (<0°C) on October 13–14. A highly anomalous snow fell in the higher elevations on October 16. Maximum temperatures during November had the largest departures of the year with readings more than 7°F (4°C) above normal, but December brought near seasonal readings. A cold snap at mid-month did bring some minimums below 10°F (-12°C).

Overall, the annual temperature for 2009 averaged near normal (Table 4). The total growing season length (days between last spring freeze and first fall freeze) ranged from 124–170 days in 2009, near the long-term average (Table 2).

Table 2. Status of 2009 temperature indicators compared to the 30-year normal (1971–2000) at the Matamoras (MATP1), Hawley (HAWP1), and Pleasant Mount (PLEP1) stations.

Temperature Indicator	Matamoras, PA 2009	Matamoras, PA 1971–2000	Hawley, PA 2009	Hawley, PA 1971–2000	Pleasant Mount, PA 2009	Pleasant Mount, PA 1971–2000
Average Annual Temperature	47.6°F 8.7°C	49.5°F 9.7°C	45.8°F 7.7°C	46.8°F 8.2°C	43.5°F 6.4°C	43.3°F 6.3°C
Average Annual Maximum Temperature	58.2°F 14.6°C	60.5°F 15.8°C	56.6°F 13.7°C	58.1°F 14.5°C	53.0°F 11.7°C	53.5°F 11.9°C
Summer Maximum (highest temperature) (°F)	91.0°F 32.8°C	94.6°F 34.8°C	93.0°F 33.9°C	91.0°F 32.8°C	86.0°F 30.0°C	87.9°F 31.1°C
Hot Days (days with Tmax≥90°F/32°C)	1	11	2	4	0	0
Average Annual Minimum Temperature (°F)	37.1°F 2.8°C	38.5°F 3.6°C	35.1°F 1.7°C	35.4°F 1.9°C	34.3°F 1.3°C	33.1°F 0.6°C
Winter Minimum (lowest temperature) (°F)	-12.0°F -24.4°C	-5.6°F -20.9°C	-15.0°F -26.1°C	-11.4°F -24.1°C	-14.0°F -25.6°C	-14.6°F -25.9°C
Cold Days (days with Tmax≤32°F/0°F)	46	27	53	37	67	63
Sub-freezing Nights (days with Tmin≤32°F/0°C)	147	132	154	159	159	174
Cold Winter Nights (days with Tmin≤0°F/-17.8°C)	5	4	12	11	6	16
Growing Season Length (days between last spring 32°F/0°C and first fall 32°F/0°C)	170	165	145	145	124	130

Delaware Water Gap National Recreation Area
and Upper Delaware Scenic and Recreational River
Departure from Average Monthly Maximum Temperature
2009 vs. 1971–2000

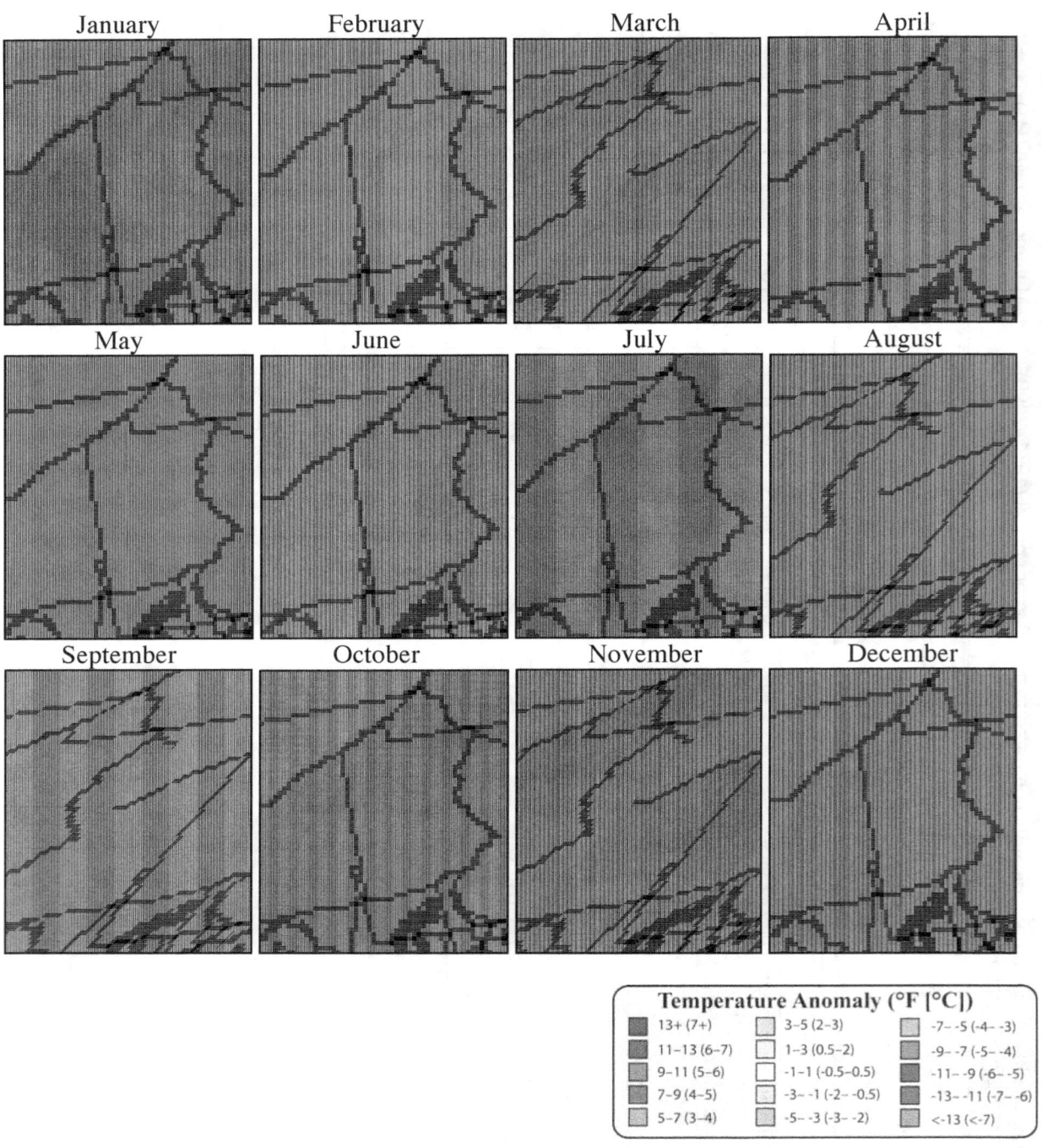

Figure 2. Maps showing departure from average monthly maximum temperature compared to the 30-year normal (1971–2000).

Delaware Water Gap National Recreation Area
and Upper Delaware Scenic and Recreational River
Departure from Average Monthly Minimum Temperature
2009 vs. 1971–2000

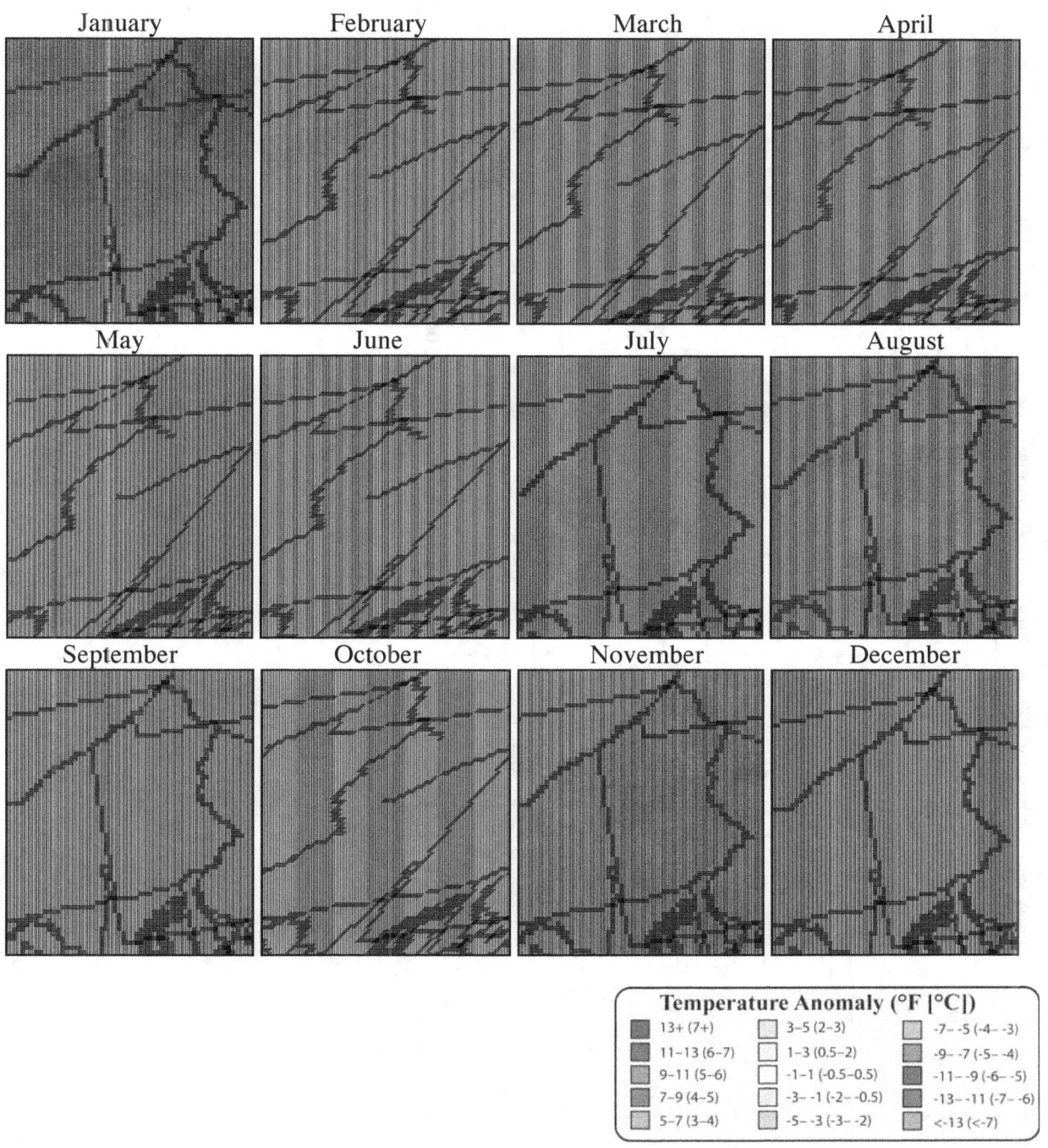

Figure 3. Maps showing departure from average monthly minimum temperature compared to the 30-year normal (1971–2000).

Table 3. Summary of monthly average temperature for 2009 for the selected stations.

Station name	Station	Jan	Feb	Mar	Apr	May	Jun	Jul	Aug	Sep	Oct	Nov	Dec	Annual
Matamoras, PA	MATP1	18.4°F	27.3°F	35.6°F	47.9°F	57.0°F	65.2°F	67.0°F	70.3°F	60.3°F	48.6°F	44.8°F	28.6°F	47.6°F
		-7.6°C	-2.6°C	2.0°C	8.8°C	13.9°C	18.4°C	19.5°C	21.3°C	15.7°C	9.2°C	7.1°C	-1.9°C	8.7°C
Hawley, PA	HAWP1	15.7°F	26.0°F	34.9°F	47.2°F	55.6°F	63.5°F	65.5°F	68.5°F	58.3°F	45.9°F	42.9°F	26.0°F	45.8°F
		-9.1°C	-3.3°C	1.6°C	8.4°C	13.1°C	17.5°C	18.6°C	20.3°C	14.6°C	7.7°C	6.1°C	-3.4°C	7.7°C
Rock Hill, NY	RKHN6	17.0°F	26.2°F	34.3°F	47.3°F	55.7°F	63.5°F	65.7°F	69.1°F	58.3°F	46.5°F	43.1°F	25.6°F	46.0°F
		-8.3°C	-3.2°C	1.3°C	8.5°C	13.2°C	17.5°C	18.7°C	20.6°C	14.6°C	8.1°C	6.2°C	-3.6°C	7.8°C
Pleasant Mount, PA	PLEP1	14.0°F	23.5°F	31.4°F	44.7°F	52.8°F	60.8°F	62.8°F	66.1°F	56.6°F	44.3°F	41.1°F	24.4°F	43.5°F
		-10.0°C	-4.7°C	-0.3°C	7.1°C	11.6°C	16.0°C	17.1°C	18.9°C	13.7°C	6.8°C	5.1°C	-4.2°C	6.4°C
Milanville, PA	MLAP1	M	M	35.0°F	48.3°F	56.6°F	64.4°F	66.7°F	69.5°F	59.9°F	47.5°F	44.5°F	27.5°F	M
		M	M	1.7°C	9.1°C	13.7°C	18.0°C	19.3°C	20.8°C	15.5°C	8.6°C	6.9°C	-2.5°C	M
Mount Pocono, PA	KMPO	17.9°F	27.9°F	34.9°F	47.7°F	56.0°F	62.3°F	65.2°F	68.0°F	58.3°F	47.2°F	43.2°F	26.4°F	46.3°F
		-7.8°C	-2.3°C	1.6°C	8.7°C	13.3°C	16.8°C	18.4°C	20.0°C	14.6°C	8.4°C	6.2°C	-3.1°C	7.9°C
Sussex, NJ	KFWN	21.8°F	30.3°F	38.4°F	51.1°F	58.5°F	65.0°F	68.5°F	70.6°F	60.6°F	50.0°F	44.9°F	30.1°F	49.2°F
		-5.7°C	-0.9°C	3.6°C	10.6°C	14.7°C	18.3°C	20.3°C	21.4°C	15.9°C	10.0°C	7.2°C	-1.1°C	9.5°C
Andover, NJ	K12N	23.8°F	31.1°F	38.5°F	51.0°F	59.5°F	66.5°F	68.8°F	71.9°F	61.5°F	50.2°F	45.6°F	30.8°F	49.9°F
		-4.6°C	-0.5°C	3.6°C	10.6°C	15.3°C	19.2°C	20.4°C	22.2°C	16.4°C	10.1°C	7.6°C	-0.7°C	10.0°C
Blue Mountain Lakes, NJ	TS717	19.4°F	29.0°F	36.7°F	49.8°F	57.8°F	63.0°F	66.7°F	69.0°F	59.7°F	48.5°F	44.1°F	29.0°F	47.7°F
		-7.0°C	-1.7°C	2.6°C	9.9°C	14.3°C	17.2°C	19.3°C	20.6°C	15.4°C	9.2°C	6.7°C	-1.7°C	8.7°C
Loch Lomond, PA	LOLP1	20.8°F	30.5°F	38.4°F	51.1°F	58.4°F	64.3°F	67.4°F	70.0°F	60.8°F	49.5°F	45.0°F	29.4°F	48.8°F
		-6.2°C	-0.8°C	3.6°C	10.6°C	14.7°C	17.9°C	19.7°C	21.1°C	16.0°C	9.7°C	7.2°C	-1.4°C	9.3°C

* M = missing data (Monthly statistics are reported as' M' if greater than 4 days of data are missing).

Table 4. Summary of 2009 departure from normal temperature based on 30-year normal (1971–2000) for the selected stations.

Station name	Station	Jan	Feb	Mar	Apr	May	Jun	Jul	Aug	Sep	Oct	Nov	Dec	Annual
Matamoras, PA	MATP1	-6.6°F	0.1°F	1.3°F	0.2°F	-1.5°F	-1.6°F	-4.4°F	0.3°F	-1.8°F	-2.4°F	4.5°F	-1.6°F	-1.9°F
		-3.7°C	0.0°C	0.7°C	0.1°C	-0.8°C	-0.9°C	-2.5°C	0.2°C	-1.0°C	-1.3°C	2.5°C	-0.9°C	-1.1°C
Hawley, PA	HAWP1	-7.5°F	1.0°F	0.7°F	2.3°F	-0.1°F	-0.3°F	-2.9°F	1.6°F	-1.1°F	-2.7°F	3.9°F	-2.5°F	-1.0°F
		-4.2°C	0.6°C	0.4°C	1.3°C	-0.1°C	-0.2°C	-1.6°C	0.9°C	-0.6°C	-1.5°C	2.2°C	-1.4°C	-0.6°C
Pleasant Mount, PA	PLEP1	-4.9°F	2.7°F	2.0°F	3.6°F	0.3°F	-0.1°F	-2.5°F	2.4°F	0.9°F	-0.6°F	6.1°F	0.2°F	0.2°F
		-2.7°C	1.5°C	1.1°C	2.0°C	0.2°C	-0.1°C	-1.4°C	1.3°C	0.5°C	-0.3°C	3.4°C	0.1°C	0.1°C
Mount Pocono, PA	KMPO	-4.2°F	5.0°F	3.1°F	4.7°F	2.3°F	-0.3°F	-1.5°F	2.8°F	0.9°F	-0.3°F	6.4°F	-0.3°F	1.6°F
		-2.3°C	2.8°C	1.7°C	2.6°C	1.3°C	-0.2°C	-0.8°C	1.6°C	0.5°C	-0.2°C	3.6°C	-0.2°C	0.9°C
Sussex, NJ	KFWN	-4.7°F	1.7°F	-0.1°F	1.9°F	-0.7°F	-1.3°F	-4.2°F	1.0°F	-1.4°F	-1.6°F	4.7°F	-2.6°F	-0.6°F
		-1.4°C	1.9°C	1.1°C	2.2°C	0.4°C	-0.6°C	-1.5°C	0.7°C	-0.4°C	0.0°C	2.6°C	0.0°C	-0.3°C
Andover, NJ	K12N	-1.1°F	3.6°F	1.8°F	3.5°F	1.5°F	-0.1°F	-2.5°F	2.6°F	0.1°F	-0.4°F	5.1°F	0.5°F	1.2°F
		-0.6°C	2.2°C	1.0°C	1.9°C	0.8°C	-0.1°C	-1.4°C	1.4°C	0.1°C	-0.2°C	2.8°C	0.3°C	0.7°C

*Indicates a station's period of record is less than 30 years. In these cases, the departure from normal values were calculated with normals derived from data spanning the length of the station's period of record. Stations with a period of record of less than 5 years were not included in this table.

Table 5. Seasonal temperature and precipitation rankings over 115 years (1 = warmest/wettest year and 115 = coldest/driest year) for Pennsylvania Climate Division 1 (top), New Jersey Climate Division 1 (middle), and New York Climate Division 2 (bottom).

PA Climate Division 1 Rankings "Pocono Mountains"	Jan–Feb–Mar WINTER	Apr–May–Jun SPRING	Jul–Aug–Sep SUMMER	Oct–Nov–Dec AUTUMN
Temperature-2009	54	27	73	44
Precipitation-2009	113	17	34	48

NJ Climate Division 1 Rankings "Northern NJ"	Jan–Feb–Mar WINTER	Apr–May–Jun SPRING	Jul–Aug–Sep SUMMER	Oct–Nov–Dec AUTUMN
Temperature-2009	41	30	45	23
Precipitation-2009	115	14	36	22

NY Climate Division 2 Rankings "Eastern Plateau"	Jan–Feb–Mar WINTER	Apr–May–Jun SPRING	Jul–Aug–Sep SUMMER	Oct–Nov–Dec AUTUMN
Temperature-2009	60	41	96	37
Precipitation-2009	96	23	9	38

Precipitation Summary

For the ninth consecutive year, annual precipitation (rain and melted snow, ice, sleet, etc.; hereafter precipitation) for calendar year 2009 averaged above the long-term mean (Table 6). Differing from the trend of recent years, the majority of the wettest days occurred during the warmer half of the year (Table 7). The months of June, July, August, October, and December averaged above normal precipitation throughout the region (Figure 4; Tables 8 and 9). The highest accumulated liquid occurred in June, July, and August (Table 8). Dry spells were noted in early August and September, which is typical, but also in January, March, and November (Table 7). Snowfall was very close to normal, due, in large part, to a snowy December. The number of days with excessive rainfall (>1.0 in [25 mm]) was below the long-term average for northeastern Pennsylvania (Table 6).

The year began with one of the driest first 100 days of any year (Figure 4; Tables 8 and 9) and was one of the driest in the past 115 years (Table 5). By the middle of April, most of the park areas had received less than 65% of the normal rainfall (Table 9), which translates to less than 4 in (100 mm). The wettest time occurred during the last week of March and the first week of April when some areas tallied more than 2.0 in (550 mm). Snowfall came in three major disturbances on January 18–19, February 3–4, and March 2–3.

Spring 2009 (April–May–June) started very dry, but turned quite wet (Tables 8 and 9). The period from May 24 until July 4 (41 days) had only nine days without any rain. June averaged the wettest month of the year with total rainfall ranging from 3.9 in (100 mm) to as much as 8.9 in (230 mm) (Tables 8 and 9).

The summer brought above-average rainfall with two of the three months tallying more than 150% of normal (Table 9). September turned quite dry with the longest dry spell of the year beginning on August 31 and persisting until September 10 (Table 7). There were no direct effects of any tropical storms, though Hurricane Bill, passing well offshore, did induce some thunderstorms across the region in late August.

The autumn was wetter than normal due to a moist October and December (Tables 6, 8, and 9). November was very dry with most sections averaging less than 50% of the normal rainfall (Table 9). An unusually early wet snow fell on the higher elevations on October 16. A series of winter storms brought early snowfall to the region from December 9–20. The lower Delaware Valley (south of Delaware Water Gap NRA) recorded its greatest December snow of record on December 19–20, but the upper Delaware Valley only received a few inches (2.5–6.0 cm).

Table 6. Status of 2009 precipitation indicators compared to the 30-year normal (1971–2000) at the Matamoras (MATP1), Hawley (HAWP1), and Pleasant Mount (PLEP1) stations.

Precipitation Indicator	Matamoras, PA 2009	Matamoras, PA 1971–2000	Hawley, PA 2009	Hawley, PA 1971–2000	Pleasant Mount, PA 2009	Pleasant Mount, PA 1971–2000
Annual Precipitation	44.2 in 1,123 mm	42.1 in 1,069 mm	45.6 in 1,158 mm	40.9 in 1,039 mm	51.5 in 1,308 mm	48.4 in 1,229 mm
Autumn (Oct, Nov, Dec) Precipitation	11.9 in 302 mm	9.9 in 252 mm	10.3 in 262 mm	9.5 in 241 mm	10.6 in 269 mm	12.0 in 305 mm
Heavy Rain (days with ≥1.0 in (25 mm) rain)	8	11	8	9	10	11
Extreme Rain (days with ≥2.0 in (51 mm) rain)	0	2	1	1	0	1
Micro-drought (strings of 7+ days without rain)	5	5	6	5	5	5
Annual Snowfall	34.6 in 879 mm	32.1 in 815 mm	46.0 in 1,168 mm	43.9 in 1,115 mm	43.1 in 1,095 mm	71.7 in 1,821 mm
Snow (days with ≥0.1 in (0.3 cm) snow)	29	15	25	22	32	31
Moderate Snow (days with ≥2.0 in (5.0 cm) snow)	6	5	9	8	8	14
Heavy Snow (days with ≥5.0 in (12.7 cm) snow)	1	1	1	2	0	3

Table 7. Top five wettest days and top five dry spells (consecutive days with a trace or less of rainfall) during 2009 from the Matamoras (MATP1) station.

Wettest Days in 2009	Dry Spells in 2009
Jul. 30: 1.7 in (43 mm)	Aug. 31–Sept. 10
Nov. 20: 1.4 in (36 mm)	Jan. 20–Jan. 27
Dec. 3: 1.4 in (36 mm)	Jul. 31–Aug. 6
May 17: 1.1 in (28 mm)	Mar. 13–19
Jun. 9: 1.1 in (28 mm)	Nov. 7–13

Delaware Water Gap National Recreation Area
and Upper Delaware Scenic and Recreational River
Percent of Average Monthly Precipitation
2009 vs. 1971–2000

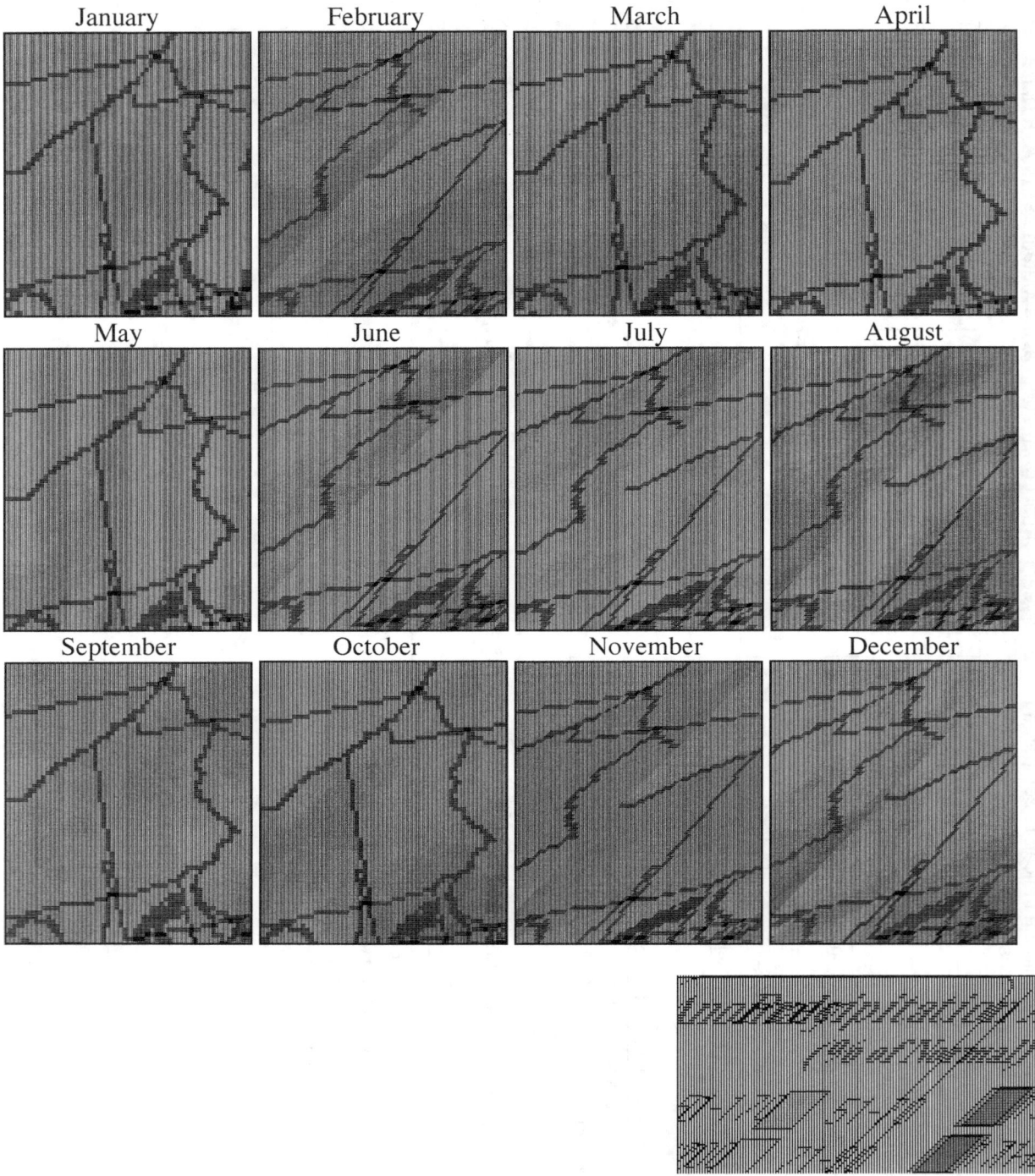

Figure 4. Maps showing percent of average monthly precipitation compared to the 30-year normal (1971–2000).

Table 8. Summary of 2009 monthly total precipitation for selected stations.

Station name	Station	Jan	Feb	Mar	Apr	May	Jun	Jul	Aug	Sep	Oct	Nov	Dec	Annual
Matamoras, PA	MATP1	2.5 in	1.0 in	2.3 in	2.9 in	3.9 in	7.7 in	5.4 in	4.5 in	2.0 in	4.7 in	1.9 in	5.3 in	44.2 in
		64 mm	25 mm	58 mm	74 mm	99 mm	196 mm	137 mm	114 mm	51 mm	119 mm	48 mm	135 mm	1,123 mm
Equinunk, PA	EQNP1	3.3 in	1.5 in	2.7 in	2.3 in	5.8 in	6.0 in	4.9 in	6.3 in	2.3 in	4.4 in	1.1 in	3.4 in	43.0 in
		84 mm	38 mm	69 mm	58 mm	147 mm	152 mm	125 mm	160 mm	58 mm	112 mm	28 mm	86 mm	1,113 mm
Hawley, PA	HAWP1	3.2 in	1.3 in	1.9 in	2.4 in	5.2 in	8.8 in	4.3 in	6.0 in	2.2 in	4.3 in	1.2 in	4.7 in	45.6 in
		81 mm	33 mm	48 mm	61 mm	132 mm	224 mm	109 mm	152 mm	56 mm	109 mm	31 mm	119 mm	1,158 mm
Rock Hill, NY	RKHN6	3.1 in	1.6 in	2.4 in	2.9 in	4.8 in	8.9 in	8.0 in	7.4 in	2.3 in	4.2 in	2.2 in	6.3 in	54.0 in
		79 mm	41 mm	61 mm	74 mm	122 mm	226 mm	203 mm	188 mm	58 mm	107 mm	56 mm	160 mm	1,372 mm
Fish's Eddy, NY	FSHN6	2.3 in	0.8 in	1.9 in	1.1 in	3.4 in	3.9 in	4.3 in	3.8 in	1.8 in	4.3 in	1.4 in	3.4 in	32.5 in
		58 mm	20 mm	48 mm	28 mm	86 mm	99 mm	109 mm	97 mm	46 mm	109 mm	36 mm	86 mm	826 mm
Pleasant Mount, PA	PLEP1	3.2 in	1.8 in	2.4 in	2.7 in	7.2 in	5.4 in	7.4 in	7.8 in	3.0 in	4.8 in	1.9 in	3.9 in	51.5 in
		81 mm	46 mm	61 mm	67 mm	183 mm	137 mm	188 mm	198 mm	76 mm	122 mm	48 mm	99 mm	1,308 mm
Milanville, PA	MLAP1	M	M	2.7 in	1.8 in	5.3 in	7.6 in	5.2 in	9.2 in	2.6 in	4.7 in	1.4 in	3.5 in	M
		M	M	69 mm	46 mm	135 mm	193 mm	132 mm	234 mm	66 mm	119 mm	36 mm	89 mm	M
Mount Pocono, PA	KMPO	1.1 in	0.9 in	1.8 in	3.6 in	4.3 in	7.5 in	5.9 in	6.0 in	2.7 in	5.3 in	2.1 in	6.7 in	47.8 in
		29 mm	22 mm	46 mm	91 mm	110 mm	191 mm	149 mm	152 mm	68 mm	135 mm	52 mm	169 mm	1,214 mm
Sussex, NJ	KFWN	2.5 in	0.7 in	1.9 in	2.6 in	3.9 in	7.9 in	6.2 in	5.3 in	1.7 in	5.6 in	1.4 in	5.6 in	45.4 in
		63 mm	19 mm	47 mm	67 mm	100 mm	201 mm	158 mm	134 mm	43 mm	143 mm	35 mm	143 mm	1,153 mm
Andover, NJ	K12N	2.2 in	0.9 in	2.6 in	2.3 in	5.1 in	4.9 in	4.1 in	7.1 in	2.0 in	4.7 in	1.0 in	6.2 in	43.0 in
		56 mm	23 mm	66 mm	58 mm	130 mm	125 mm	104 mm	180 mm	51 mm	119 mm	25 mm	158 mm	1,092 mm

* M = missing data (Monthly statistics are reported as 'M' if more than 4 days of data are missing).

Table 9. Summary of 2009 percent of normal precipitation based on 30-year normal (1971–2000) for selected stations.

Station name	Station	Jan	Feb	Mar	Apr	May	Jun	Jul	Aug	Sep	Oct	Nov	Dec	Annual
Matamoras, PA	MATP1	72	35	65	70	93	174	129	123	44	138	51	156	105
Equinunk, PA	EQNP1	96	56	75	63	143	149	131	169	57	127	27	95	100
Hawley, PA	HAWP1	101	50	62	64	129	208	119	173	58	137	33	152	111
Rock Hill, NY	RKHN6	83	52	57	68	95	187	203	194	50	111	52	167	109
Pleasant Mount, PA	PLEP1	94	63	69	65	146	111	169	190	66	115	44	107	106
Mount Pocono, PA*	KMPO	29	26	45	84	93	166	144	151	53	141	49	185	97
Sussex, NJ*	KFWN	66	25	49	61	88	174	145	130	38	148	37	156	95
Andover, NJ*	K12N	62	33	70	57	115	108	93	160	44	130	26	180	90

*Indicates a station's period of record is less than 30 years. In these cases, the departure from normal values were calculated with normals derived from data spanning the length of the station's period of record. Stations with a period of record of less than 5 years were not included in this table.

Drought Status .

There are a number of drought indices used to estimate the severity of drought in an area using algorithms that incorporate recent temperatures, rainfall, soil moisture, and other information (http://www.drought.gov). The main indices we report are the Palmer Drought Severity Index (PDSI) and the United States Drought Monitor (DM) – Drought Intensity Index. While both indices provides excellent summary information on broad-scale conditions, local conditions (such as at the park scale) may vary.

The PDSI is a soil moisture algorithm calibrated for relatively homogeneous regions and is calculated on a monthly basis using precipitation and temperature data, as well as the water content of the soil. The values vary between extremely moist (>4.0) and extreme drought (<-4.0) with "normal" values ranging between -1.9 and 1.9. Monthly PDSI values for Pennsylvania Climate Division 1 in 2009 are shown in Figure 5.

The DM – Drought Intensity Index is a synthesis of multiple indices (including the PDSI) and impacts and represents a consensus of federal and academic scientists. The DM produces a summary map of drought intensity for the nation and all states each week. It is on a scale ranging from abnormally dry (D0) to exceptional drought (D4). Mid-month (i.e., the second or third week) values for Pennsylvania (Figure 6) and the Northeast (Figure 7) are shown for 2009.

According to the PDSI for PA Climate Division 1, a dry winter grew into an early spring "moderate drought" (PDSI < -2.0; Figure 5). However, rather wet conditions in May alleviated the drought and it remained more "moist" than normal (PDSI > 0) for the summer and autumn. When compared with the past few years, 2009 was similar to 2007, though the dry spell in that year occurred during the heart of the growing season from May to September. The DM – Drought Severity Index for Pennsylvania (Figure 6) and the Northeast (Figure 7) shows a similar pattern for the growing season (May through October); abnormally dry (D0) only during the beginning of May.

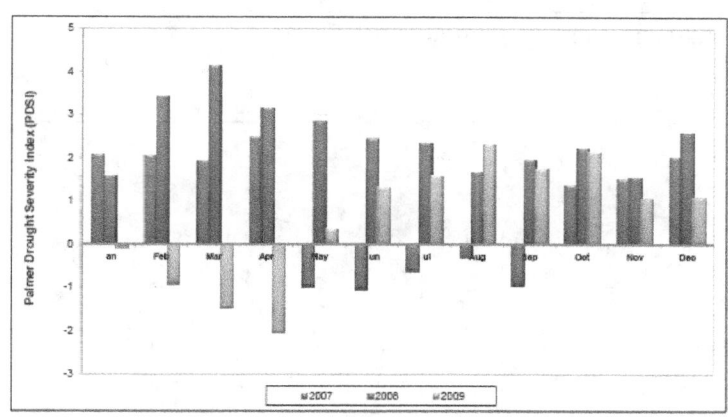

Figure 5. Monthly Palmer Drought Severity Index (PDSI) values for Pennsylvania Climate Division 1, 2007–2009.

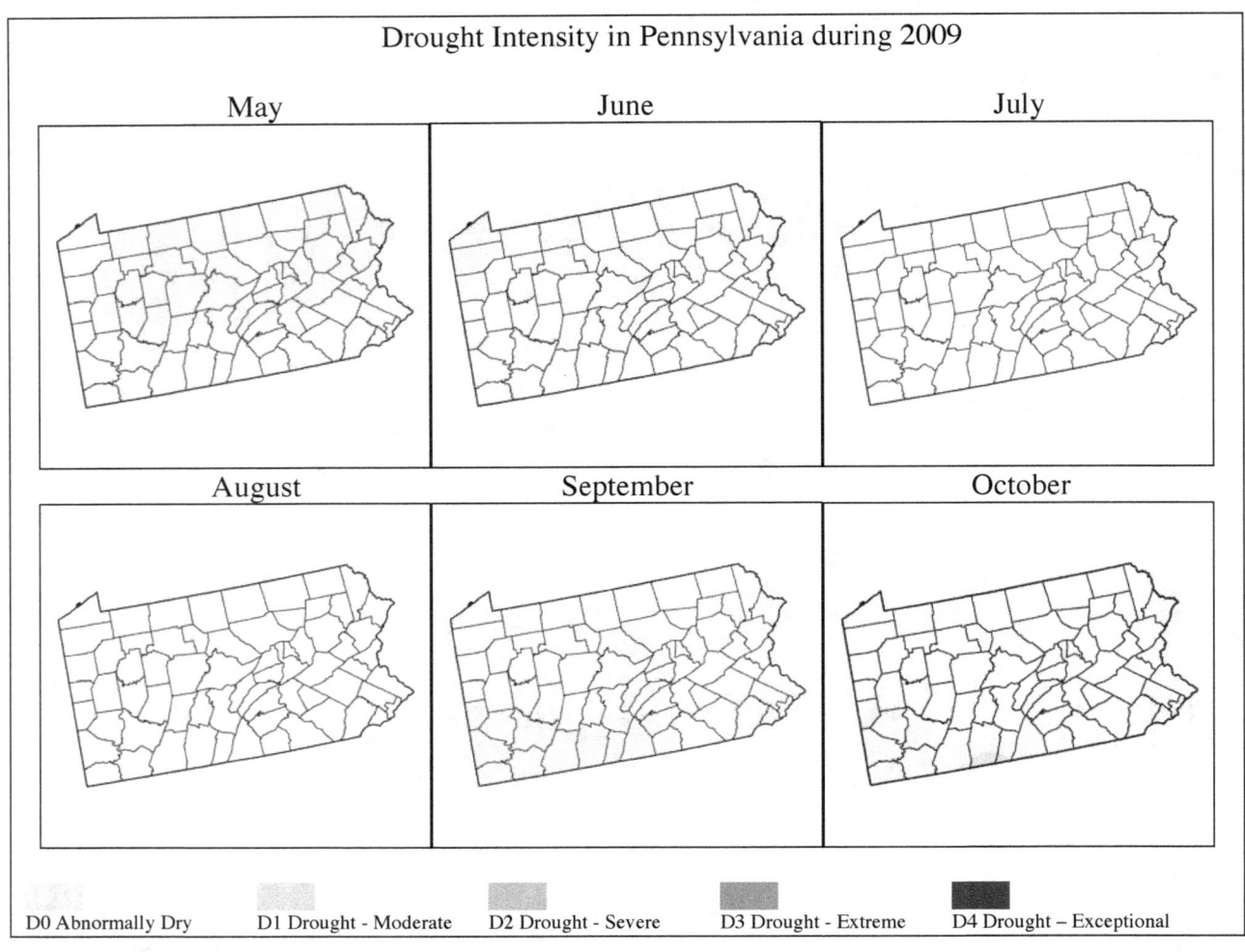

Figure 6. Mid-month values of the Drought Monitor – Drought Intensity Index for Pennsylvania in 2009.

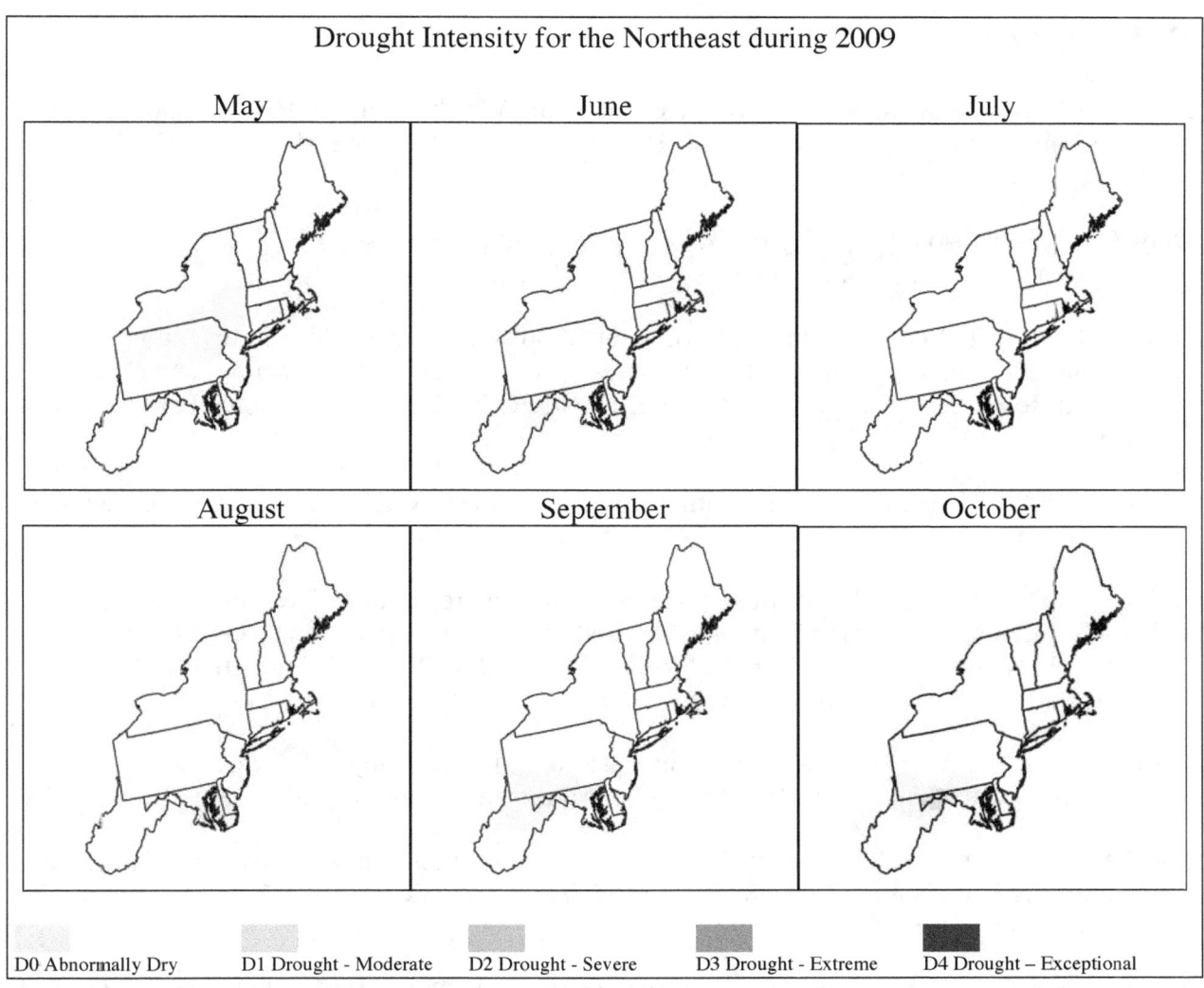

Figure 7. Mid-month values of the Drought Monitor – Drought Intensity Index for the Northeast in 2009.

References

Bureau of Land Management. 1997. Remote Automatic Weather Station (RAWS) and Remote Environmental Monitoring Systems (REMS) standards. RAWS/REMS Support Facility, Boise, Idaho.

Daly, C., W. P. Gibson, G. H. Taylor, G. L. Johnson, and P. Pasteris. 2002. A knowledge-based approach to the statistical mapping of climate. Climate Research 22:99–113.

Davey, C. A., K. T. Redmond, and D. B. Simeral. 2006. Weather and Climate Inventory. National Park Service. National Park Service, Eastern Rivers and Mountains Network. Natural Resource Technical Report NPS/ERMN/NRTR—2006/006. National Park Service, Fort Collins, CO.

Gelber, B. 2002. The Pennsylvania Weather Book. Rutgers University Press. New Brunswick, N.J.

Knight, P., T. Wisniewski, C. Bahrmann, and S. Miller. In preparation. Weather and Climate Monitoring Protocol for the Eastern Rivers and Mountains Network and Mid-Atlantic Network. Natural Resource Technical Report Series NPS/ERMN/NRR—2010/XXX. National Park Service, Fort Collins, Colorado.

Kocin, P. J., and L. W. Uccellini. 2004. Northeast Snowstorms Volume 1: Overview. Meteorological Monographs. Vol 32. No 54. American Meteorological Society. Boston, MA.

Marshall, M. R., and N. B. Piekielek. 2007. Eastern Rivers and Mountains Network Ecological Monitoring Plan. Natural Resource Report NPS/ERMN/NRR—2007/017. National Park Service. Fort Collins, CO.

National Oceanic and Atmospheric Administration (NOAA). 2008. National Climatic Data Center. Climate of 2008 – Annual Review, Global and U.S. Summary. http://lwf.ncdc.noaa.gov/oa/climate/research/2008/ann/us-summary.html.

NPS 620/105524, 647/105524, September 2010